SOLD
-ON-
SALES

TIPS, TOOLS, AND TECHNIQUES FOR
ASPIRING ENTREPRENEURS

JET ABUDA-SISON

Testimonials for Sold on Sales

"As I was learning the habits and skills of becoming successful in sales, it was Jet who I had in mind all the time. I imitated her shamelessly which made me develop my character more!" -*Gigi A.*

"I set my standards by using Jet as my role model." -*Grace B.*

"The manner in which Jet operates her business is admirable." -*Aron D.*

"Jet has managed to create a true business that holds integrity and ethics as a priority to its clients." -*Arath L.*

"You [Jet] have not only provided knowledge, information, expertise and advice, but your dedication and passion for what you do is beyond what I could have expected or asked for." -*Beth M.*

"Jet's ability to move up and down with the past, present, and future economy truly portrays her excellent flexibility in the business world." -*Long E.*

"Jet identifies her goals and takes initiative and effort to seek them through. She always has a good attitude, displays skilled conduct, and is focused on achieving her various objectives." -*Marieta U.*

"Jet is definitely a leader rather than a follower. She has proven her ability by running a successful company. I listen to whatever she has to say about sales and entrepreneurship!" -*Dan P.*

Jet Abuda-Sison/Sold on Sales
Printed in the United States of America

Sold on Sales/ Jet Abuda-Sison. -- 1st ed.

ISBN 978-1-7362390-0-1 Print Edition

ISBN 978-1-7362390-1-8 Ebook Edition

Contents

My family, team, and friends to whom without I would never be...THANK YOU!

1

The Ultimate Profession

WHEN YOU ASK KIDS what they want to be when they grow up, they have all sorts of ideas: policeman, doctor, teacher, veterinarian, astronaut. The possibilities seem to be endless. The one thing you almost never hear anyone say is, "I want to be in sales."

My question is, why?

As parents, we tend to guide our children in a different direction. Is it because we have a negative connotation brought on by a bad experience at a car dealership or an endless hard sell at a timeshare? Maybe we have tried a sales job ourselves, but failed. Maybe we consider sales too hard or too cyclical a profession to suggest to our children. Parents, friends, and society as a whole seem to want to steer people into something definitive, where there is less of the unknown than the "unproven" field of sales and entrepreneurship.

Is it because most of us do not personally know ultra-successful entrepreneurs like Elon Musk, Bill Gates, Steve

Jobs, Mark Zuckerberg, or Warren Buffet? Sure, we read about them, but becoming one of them seems farfetched. We do, however, have uncles, aunts, neighbors, cousins, friends who are doctors, lawyers, nurses, and engineers. Not only are they doing okay financially, but we can totally relate to them and have their personal testimonies. Is it because we don't have this familiarity with successful entrepreneurs that becoming one ourselves seems an impossible feat?

Most people, including me, never thought of sales as a *legitimate* career. As a young girl, I had entrepreneurial sensibilities that my mother taught me out of necessity. As for a career, I wanted to be a journalist. My dad felt journalism was too risky because the Philippines was under martial law at the time and convinced me it would be beneficial to have a doctor in the family.

Upon graduation from high school, I got accepted at the University of Santo Tomas (UST) in Manila, one of the best medical schools in the country. While I liked the idea of becoming a doctor and loved the thought of helping people, I came to realize that I was motivated in my studies by two things: I did not want to let my family down, and I wanted to do well so I would have my summers free to work as a corporate accounts manager for an international company in Manila. The challenge of making an income based totally on my own effort and creating long-term business relationships satisfied my need to succeed in a way that being a doctor could not.

Still, a career in sales seemed out of the question—it simply did not carry the same prestige. Most people equate respect to a particular profession based on the number of years it takes to get that degree. Interestingly, even though prospective physicians have no qualms about spending ten years in training to become specialists, a doctor will most likely make six to twelve million dollars in his/her entire career. It is a good living, to be sure, but if you put that much time into training in sales or becoming an entrepreneur, there is the real possibility you will greatly exceed that amount.

Because no business venture can succeed without sales, the possibility to earn money is unlimited. A very smart person can invent the best product, but without someone selling or creating a need for it, it is worth nothing.

Unfortunately, most people who try sales don't give it their all the way someone who commits to being a doctor, plumber, fireman, or any profession where they are required to take exams or work as apprentices for a specified period of time in order to be certified. So many would-be entrepreneurs only give sales a year or two, sometimes part-time, for fear of giving up the safety net of a paid job. Because there is no formal college degree in sales (although I believe there should be), people have a tendency to self-sabotage before they graduate into success. I know because I've been to the school of hard knocks, lived the self-doubt, and faced the questions from friends and family along the way.

After I got married, my husband (who was in the U.S. military) and I headed across the globe to the United States of America. We got our start in New London, Connecticut, where he was employed at one of the naval shipyards. For me, getting that first job in the States proved to be challenging. Finding a company willing to hire an immigrant without local references was not easy. I have to admit there was more than one moment where I considered going home to the Philippines to complete my studies in medicine. Thankfully, my husband received a transfer order, and instead of calling it quits, we moved to San Diego, California.

While I loved California, I was, once again, starting over—now as a young mother. I got a job working part-time for the local school district, continued taking college courses and classes focused on office procedures. Upon completion, I began to submit applications and took a position at the San Diego County Assessor's office. As I worked my way up the ladder, I learned things that were fascinating to me: how appraisals were done, how assessed values and supplemental taxes were calculated, as well as how to read parcel maps. I met people who were real estate developers and landowners. By asking questions and hearing them share their experiences, I realized that, just like the most successful business people in the Philippines, the common denominator was that they all owned real estate.

I remember calling some of the numbers on the land for sale signs in San Diego, but got total sticker shock. Not only were the prices in the millions, but they also required cash payment. With almost nothing in the form of savings, I had to put my dream of owning land on hold.

Over time, and while I was still employed at the assessor's office, a clothing business I operated on the side (from my car) evolved into an actual boutique on Plaza Boulevard in National City. I brought in new stock regularly, learned how to merchandise, budget, move inventory, and cut losses. I had overhead in the form of rent, employees, permits, insurance, government reporting, etc. I'd always dreamed of having my own business, but with a mortgage and bills and very little capital, I had to hold a steady job while I gained experience and found the industry that would work best for my family and me. Despite the headaches, stress, and time investment inherent in operating a boutique, I had a valuable crash course on entrepreneurship.

Somehow, I was able to manage the boutique, do word processing for small businesses, work at the assessor's office, and write commentaries for a local Filipino newspaper. I also received invitations to speak at community events, including swearing-in ceremonies for new citizens. Little did I know, those speeches would supplement my training for my future sales presentations.

Of all the part-time businesses I tried, I found that I enjoyed real estate the most. I particularly enjoyed selling resort membership on weekends. It wasn't long before I was making in one day what I made in a month at my full-time job. The ability to earn an income depending on the effort I put in and having the flexibility to take my kids to work on weekends, convinced me to accept a marketing director position at the resort. After ten years of proudly serving the San Diego County Assessor's office, I sold the clothing boutique and took early retirement from my job to fully dedicate my time to making the venture a success.

As the owners began to develop the residences in phases, I managed agents selling memberships to people from all over the country. Memberships sold faster than the number of units being built, but due to the economic conditions at that time, the owners were having a difficult time getting a loan for the promised and scheduled development. Members started complaining about the delay. Needless to say, there was just too much negative publicity for the project to rebound, and it spiraled downward. I watched helplessly as a project I completely believed in—a venture that brought fun and camaraderie—eventually closed.

I was bitterly disappointed and remember it as one of the darker times in my life, but, soon after, I was offered a position with a real estate company. After I researched the business thoroughly, I concluded they were reputable, established, and offered a product that I'd always dreamt of owning, and struck me as the most sensible: land.

I took the leap and became their marketing director.

I now had the opportunity to help people become landowners. It was a challenge I enjoyed taking on. I had to build a sales force from scratch. I developed a presentation based on what I would want and need to know if I were the potential client, and then modified it based on my audience.

After a few years, I understood how most land companies operated, but felt that the business model my company offered didn't always suit everyone's needs. I wanted to offer clients the opportunity to own land in varying locations, and in a variety of sizes, to suit their particular goals. I was certain that I simply needed to understand where the next areas of development were likely to happen. Because this was not a viable option where I worked, I considered starting my own company. As an immigrant, especially one who'd had enough setbacks to understand it took time, effort, money, hard work, and even heartache to even attempt to achieve what you wanted, I never thought that I could become a landowner in America, much less own a land company.

I decided to go for it, anyway.

To my friends, including some family, I was making a grave mistake leaving the company where I worked. It was, once again, leaving a "secure" job that would give me a definite retirement. As my family and friends' opinion mattered to me, it was a time of enormous self-doubt and uncertainty. What if they were right? There was no manual or course of studies to follow. There wasn't even necessarily a how-to book for the career I was considering. Most advice was to keep my regular job and do entrepreneurship on the side. I'd already done that and had come to believe that not really giving it your all was what made most people fail. The safety net they wanted to fall back on kept them from taking the necessary risks. But, having gone through many rough patches in the past, I had become less and less afraid of taking chances. Somehow, each struggle made the next one easier to handle.

In 1999, I founded Capital Holdings.

Becoming a land sales entrepreneur has been one of the best decisions I've ever made, but the path to that decision was certainly not straightforward or easy. Being in business has its magnificent highs and devastating lows. Looking back, I would have never known the joy that I now enjoy if I backed out or quit when the going got tough. I am appreciative of the choice I made because my life's journey has been so much more colorful, fulfilling, and financially gratifying. I truly appreciate having in-depth knowledge and understanding of the difference between doing what you have to do and doing what you love.

I meet a lot of people who are in sales who want to know what I did to make it in this profession. Others have already given up and have gone back to salaried jobs without putting in the necessary effort to succeed. Being an entrepreneur is not easy. If it was, there would be way more people out there doing it. Anything worth achieving takes time, dedication, and hard work.

If you are willing to learn, figure things out as you go, be persistent, and not give up, I believe sales is the very best profession. What other career offers unlimited income potential, financial independence, the chance to meet and help people from all walks of life, self- fulfillment, and the ability to manage your own time?

My hope is that by sharing my experiences, I can help someone avoid some of the missteps I've made. I realize that some of us are just doing things because that is what is expected of us and are never given the opportunity to live on the other side and know the difference. There may be an easier path to take in life, but creating your own, and being given the chance to create a new road so that others may use it, is well worth considering. The world needs more entrepreneurs, more risk-takers, more who are willing to challenge the norm. While many people may believe that becoming a doctor, a lawyer, or an engineer is the mark of success, true success is when you end up doing what you love to do.

2

Born to Sell

I BELIEVE THAT becoming a salesperson or entrepreneur is a truly misunderstood concept. People often fail to recognize and acknowledge that we are all in sales—and have been our entire lives. While some people may be more successful than others, being alive and part of society means we are always selling ourselves. We make ourselves acceptable to family, friends, classmates, potential significant others, and society in general, in countless ways: how we act, speak, dress, fix our hair, etc. We just don't think of what we are doing as selling.

The moment we are born, we are in sales. Our first customers are our parents, who are, with a few exceptions, the easiest sell, ever. Our parents already believe we are the cutest, smartest, and all-around best being ever created. Everything we do is fascinating and cute. We learn early that if we cry, they scramble to give us milk. When we fuss, we get a quick diaper change. If we give a half smile, it melts their hearts. Give them a full smile, and we fill them with sheer joy. All we have to do is be darling, and our parents are utterly and completely sold.

As I said, the simplest sale ever.

Admittedly, from here on out, things start to get a bit more complex. In other words, in order to get everything our little hearts desire, we enter a slightly more sophisticated phase of selling. If we have siblings, we start to realize we aren't the only game in town. There may be some pushback to our self-indulgent agenda because we don't have sole rights to every toy in the house. We must compete for our parents' attention. We have to learn to ask, share, negotiate, and justify why we should get to play with the object of our desire first. The more siblings, the better sales training we get.

Then, the day comes when we have to venture out from the comfort and total acceptance of family life and go to school. Here, we are exposed to classmates who may have been brought up differently and won't necessarily share our way of looking at and valuing things. This is where we start selling seriously. We often try to look for the kids who are most like us in an effort to find the easiest fit (the easy sell). But, if we want to belong to a different group, we really have to start selling by talking and dressing the part, getting better grades, and negotiating to gain acceptance. Sometimes, we even do things we shouldn't do just to belong.

As we get toward the end of our formal education, we begin selling ourselves on what we need to be and achieve.

We specialize and gain degrees for the sole purpose of a better, more comfortable life to help our family, ourselves, and our community. We set life goals. Then, we venture out into the "real world."

One of our biggest first sales is the job interview—a process of selling ourselves and our acquired skills to a company, convincing them they are in need of our expertise so they will pay a salary that allows us to enjoy the life we've envisioned.

Once we get a job, no matter what the industry, that is where our lives become a series of sales transactions. It is in this phase we now have to continuously sell our boss and coworkers on the fact that we are worth what they've agreed to pay us. We have to conform by dressing a certain way (sometimes even in a uniform), arrive and leave at a certain time, and continue to convince others of our value.

We now depend on a paycheck to sustain our way of life. We often have family to support, and it is at this point in our lives that we try to sell ourselves on the belief that we have chosen the best way. For some people, it is. There are those who like being around people, but the idea of selling them something is terrifying. That is perfectly okay. You cannot be in sales or decide to be an entrepreneur just because somebody you know is in it and doing well. If there's anything that makes this world the awesome place it is, it's the diversity and differences between us.

If, however, the idea of going into sales crosses your mind, it's worth looking into. Do you have the strength, willingness, and drive to see it through? Are you willing to pay the price? You need to go into analysis mode because conscious decision making is key.

DIPPING YOUR TOE INTO THE WARM MARKET

For those of us who may have an interest or an ability to take what we do intuitively in life and translate it into a career, there are an endless array of sales opportunities on a myriad of products: make-up, vacuums, water filters, vitamins, insurance, etc. Often, we will venture into selling something on the side for possible additional income. We tap into the easiest sales with our parents, siblings, cousins, and friends—otherwise known as a "warm" market. This warm market is typically supportive, and most of our acquaintances will buy, not necessarily because they want the product we are offering, but usually to help us out.

The dreaded day of having sold to everyone we know is often the dead end for a lot of people. Simply stated, the thought of going out of the "warm" market can be daunting. Since the "cold" (better known as the real) marketplace is filled with prospective clients who don't have an emotional investment in us to consider, and who are much more likely to turn down what we are offering, we are afraid to venture into this part of the business world.

Getting a "no" can be very devastating. A rejection can toss our opinion of sales into the abyss. Once we feel like a prospective client is saying no to us personally, some of us are toast. Rather than blaming ourselves by seeing our own lack of effort, imagination, or being too thin-skinned, we determine sales is therefore, not a good career.

This might well be the end of the outside sales journey and some people will go back to what is already familiar - that of continuously selling their boss by the quality of the job they do.

That is okay, too.

Don't trade who you really are with what others want you to be. Living a full life means doing what *you* want. It means owning the responsibility of how you will live your life. It will be your life, after all—no one else's.

No matter what your career goals and how fast you intend to meet them, the biggest goal of all is to find your purpose. What keeps you interested? What makes you happy? Working on what you are passionate about will make anything you do an interesting challenge as opposed to a task. I believe you need to take an honest assessment of yourself by answering the following questions:

1. Do you enjoy what you do together with its imperfections?

2. Do you have a happy, balanced life?

3. Do you have a clarity of purpose?

4. Do you know what you want?

5. Do you look forward to going to work every day?

If the answer to any of these questions is no and you are leaning toward a career in sales/business, congratulations! There are a select few of us who have the guts to leave what is constant and venture into the unknown. If you have an interest in being in business, why not try? Only two things will happen—you either totally succeed in your endeavor or will have a better appreciation of whatever you end up doing in life.

Either way, you win.

3

Must Have Qualities for a Successful Career in Sales

I HAVE ALWAYS BEEN fascinated with land, but it was years before I realized this deep appreciation for real estate was due at least in part to the fact that owning land had saved my family from being homeless after the fire that destroyed my childhood home. Sales were never mentioned in my family as a career option, so I started out on one path until my abilities, my love of people, and my passion for land intersected with a career that offered me joy and does to this day.

I believe there are two ways to go about a journey – be in the driver's seat, or be someone else's passenger. As a passenger, you may have more time to look and enjoy the view and, perhaps, less stress, but no control of the view. If you are in the driver's seat, you have the ability to decide where to go, how fast you should go, when to stop, and how far to go.

Having successfully switched seats, I can't imagine anyone being satisfied sitting behind a desk all day talking to no one, and beholden to his or her boss, etc. Sales and entrepreneurship is an exhilarating career, but that is because I am extremely well-suited for the demands both day-to-day and long term. To be successful, it takes a certain set of skills, some of which can be developed, and others which are innate. If you are considering a career in sales, or undertaking an entrepreneurial endeavor, you need to have or be open to developing the following traits:

PEOPLE PERSON

Sales is all about relationships, so you must enjoy being around people. If you love people, you most likely have an abundance of compassion and understanding, another key element to success in sales. If being social is hard and does not give you joy, you must accept that truth about yourself. As I've said, we are all different. Accepting, celebrating, and appreciating this fact will make your journey, no matter what you do, that much more amazing.

RESPECT FOR OTHERS

The respect you have for others is very transparent. You may think that people will not notice and feel it, but they always do. If you are uncomfortable, you will emit that vibe and that energy, and you will get the same energy right back.

I had an agent whom I assigned to take care of two clients. He seemed to cater more to the client that he thought was more capable of buying a much higher priced parcel. Both of them ended up buying that day, but the buyer for the smaller priced parcel felt underserved by my agent. He was very happy with the purchase and referred new prospective clients to us, but always to different agents than the person he worked with. He continues to do so to this day.

HIGH DOSE OF POSITIVE ATTITUDE

Positivity is a major attraction. People are attracted to people who have a can-do attitude. Nobody wants to be around a glum person. If you keep repeating what's hurting you, bothering you, or on your mind, you will begin to believe it and broadcast your negativity. If we want to hear negativity, all we have to do is turn on the news. Pessimists are a dime a dozen. Be different. Be rare.

Given all the challenges we experience in life, a positive attitude can easily erode. Good and bad things happen to everyone without exception. The difference is how we take and accept these experiences. To me, the glass is always half-full, and that's a choice. I take difficult obstacles as a challenge rather than a downer. When it's raining, people tend to be melancholy, but they don't have to be. In fact, I like the sound of the rain. You may look at challenges as burdens, or you may use them as a stepping stone towards getting what you want.

Instead of feeling disadvantaged as a foreign-born woman in a mostly male industry, I focused on the possibility people would remember me better, and immigrants would relate to me just as I did to them. I thought of these possibilities as positives and was able to use them to my advantage.

SELF-MOTIVATION

Are you a self-starter? Does the idea of having a self-directed sense of purpose sound exhilarating or exhausting? Will you be able to show up for work without anybody telling you to be in at nine and go home at five? When you're self-employed, you're not accountable to anyone other than yourself. You are the boss because your income depends on your productivity. To be successful in sales or as an entrepreneur, you have to be a self-starter and be able to sustain your motivation.

I pretty much treat myself as my employee. I've been known to ask myself, *would I hire Jet? Is she dependable, accountable, and honorable? Would I hire her again?* My husband thinks I'm absolutely crazy when I say such things out loud, but if I don't give myself an honest review, who is going to? When you start lying to yourself, you self-sabotage whatever success you could have. You have to be able to be accountable to yourself.

If you love what you do, however, motivation comes easy. You will forever have that fire in your belly. There will be little need to gas up all the time.

RISK AVERSION

The opportunity to succeed in sales is determined by the amount of risk you are willing to take. The thing that discourages people most from embarking on a sales career is the uncertainty or lack of guarantee provided by a steady paycheck. However, we've all seen big corporations fold and close. Because of the current pandemic and economic recession, multiple "safe" employers have laid people off and shut down. Still, entrepreneurship is about taking risks. Are you willing to put your own money and resources into your goal as opposed to someone else's money? The more risks you take, the more chances of winning. You have to have a willingness, even an eagerness, to take chances. We all know there are no guarantees in life, but if you are truly risk-averse, sales is not for you.

DETERMINATION/PERSISTENCE

I have met successful people in various fields. I will often ask them about how they made it. The more I dig, the more obvious it is that there are no shortcuts to success in anything. It is easy to look at somebody and admire them for their "luck," but aside from winning the lottery, there is no such thing. Even winning the lottery requires going to the store, buying the ticket, and having the money to pay for the ticket in the first place. Luck simply becomes more achievable with hard work.

How much effort and sacrifice are you willing to put into what you want to achieve? Determination is something many people lose too easily in sales. A negative comment is sometimes all it takes for some to give up. Success in anything we do is directly proportional to the number of rejections, failures, and challenges we've faced to get there. The point is, everything takes effort, and it takes a lot of practice to be the best and to be your best self. You must be ready for challenges and hard work. Anything worth achieving takes time and dedication.

FLEXIBILITY

How do you adjust and conform to situations? Can you compartmentalize when necessary? Flexibility and an ability to go with the flow is a necessity in this world. Being rigid will make you break easily. It is best to be like liquid that follows the contour of wherever it is contained. You have to be able to handle ups and downs, and there *will* be ups and downs. There will be mighty falls, and you've got to be able to gather yourself, dust yourself off, and do it again.

INTEGRITY/DEPENDABILITY

No matter how large or small the deal, people have to be able to take your word. You should not promise things that you can't deliver. Just because it is not in a written, notarized, or a signed contract, if you promised it, you've got to do it! If at all possible, you need to over-deliver on what you promise.

When clients ask for directions to their parcel, no matter how long ago they purchased it from the company, we not only provide a map, clear direction, and coordinates; we offer to take them there ourselves. Doing this has resulted in more referrals and repeat sales over the years.

CONFIDENCE

A good salesperson is confident. Confidence is usually an aura a person possesses having gone through challenges and succeeded—meaning confidence can be learned. Sometimes we all have to fake it until we make it. If you gain a thorough knowledge of your product, confidence will be automatic. If in your heart, you know you are confident or have the ability to exude this important quality, you are well suited to a career in sales.

ABILITY TO NETWORK

You need to enjoy meeting people, creating business relationships, and becoming involved in organizations that lend themselves to your goals and aspirations. Communication skills and the ability to convey what you want to say for people to follow you is a must. Words have power. Being able to communicate in front of an audience is crucial, so always find ways to improve your writing and speaking skills.

I get invited to speak about real estate and entrepreneurship because of the years of knowledge and experience I've attained over the years. This makes networking easy for me. Others gauge the confidence I have in delivering the information I share, which expands my client and referral base. When you know what you're talking about, people want to talk to you, making networking easier.

SENSE OF PURPOSE

When I started my company, and up to this day, my main objective and purpose is to give people the opportunity to own affordable land in a developing area. It is therefore, up to me to give the information and understanding that people will need to see it the way I do.

Even if I know that a client may not be ready to make a decision that day or only one showed up, I will always do my best. Nothing makes me happier than being of help and benefit to others.

In order to succeed in sales, you need to have or develop a love for the game. If you enjoy being with people, love what you do, and have a thorough knowledge of your product, you're well on your way.

Are you still with me? Do you feel like you might just have what it takes to move to the next step? If so, let's move on to figuring out what business or industry best suits your personality, interests, and abilities.

4

What Kind of Business or Industry?

I HAVE ALWAYS UNDERSTOOD and appreciated the value of land. My parents were amongst the lucky few who owned a small bit of acreage back home in the Philippines. As a result, they were able to pawn and redeem it as needed to be able to send my siblings and me to college.

However, I wondered how, if my family could not afford to buy any more land in the Philippines beyond what we already had, could I, an immigrant, possibly afford to own anything in the United States? Especially in Southern California, and, more specifically, San Diego, where I lived?

I truly believed owning land in the richest country in the world was just too farfetched for an immigrant like me. Going into the land business was unthinkable.

I was also very wrong.

To start, I made a number of false assumptions. For one thing, I thought land in America, the richest country in the world, was likely to be very expensive. In my mind, it had to be hundreds of times more costly than a developing country like the Philippines. At that time, I didn't understand that the cost of land is tied to both availability and population. The Philippines, about thirty-three times smaller than the U.S., or 3.05% the size of the United States, has a population of over 109 million, while the United States has a population of approximately 337 million people spread out across a vast distance of varied terrain and usability. As a result, farmlands in the Philippines can be far more expensive than farmlands here in the U.S. (https://www.mylifeelsewhere.com)

When I started working at the San Diego Assessor's office, I had the opportunity to meet and talk to some of the county's big taxpayers. One thing I noticed they had in common was that most had invested in and developed land. At that time, I thought of land ownership as involving traditional housing and commercial development but learned that no matter where you are in the world, everything begins with land. You live in a house on land, your place of work sits on land, the food you eat is grown on land, etc. Soon, solar power would be a mandate in California, and land would be needed to harness the sun.

I began to realize that my interest in owning land had been an enduring passion and that I wanted to explore real estate sales as a career. After passing my broker's exam, I went into analysis mode. There are many facets in real estate: commercial real estate, leasing, property management, mortgage, and land. As a broker, you can do any or all of it. I was leaning toward land and its universal value as opposed to more traditional real estate. Selling land had many challenges, though. Home purchases were financed by banks. Many industries benefit from home sales: cement, steel, roofing, wood, fabric, etc. Once homes are purchased, homeowners make endless trips to Walmart, Target, Home Depot, and Lowe's, which is good for the economy. With the availability of financing, buying a home has always been the norm. Raw land, however, was mostly financed by owners who were selling to basically cash out. I discovered that land purchases were rarely financed by banks and only when leveraged towards their advantage via construction loans.

As a result, land was only truly affordable to those with deep pockets. For someone like me, a new immigrant, who did not have the financial resource, it felt out of reach. This lack of access for regular people who wanted to own land is exactly what inspired me.

I formed my business on the concept that we all know how valuable land is, how it can benefit us in the future, and how we want it for ourselves and our children. But, because many people don't really understand where and how to buy land, I would help them answer those questions. More important, I would figure out how to offer affordable financing that would make land ownership available to many.

It took a long process to find a location that was both affordable and poised for growth. In San Bernardino County, for instance, 81% of the land is owned by the government, so supply and demand is an advantage. I bought up all the land I could in bulk because I only wanted to sell a product I owned and knew well.

I went through a long process to figure out what I wanted and was meant to do, but I believe I can shorten the process for those who feel like their path to finding their passion may be in sales and entrepreneurship.

To do so, ask yourself the following, all-important question: **what interests me?**

WHAT IS YOUR PASSION?

1. Is it the food industry? Is it the service business? Real Estate? Technology?

2. In what specific segment of this industry do you see yourself?

For instance, if you choose real estate, there are various aspects in real estate to choose from: mortgage, property management, home sales, commercial leasing, land, etc. For me, narrowing my choice down to land and not mixing it with anything else allowed me to focus on exactly where I could do the most good and be the most successful.

3. **Once you narrow down the industry that interests you, if at all possible, work, volunteer, or do apprentice work in that industry.** This will help you solidify your choice and, potentially, minimize your eventual start-up costs.

4. **Zone in and learn as much as you can.** Be very objective. See the positive but get clarity on the problem areas to determine if you have the capability and willingness to take them on.

5. **Research the people who have made it in your prospective field and learn how and why they are at the top.** Reading up on people who have failed is just as important as knowing who has succeeded because you need to know what not to do, and why. Many successful people are willing to share - you simply have to ask! It is easy to get intimidated and think that they will not have time to teach, but remember successful people are often great teachers. Ask questions, be discerning, be curious, investigate, and research.

CHOOSING YOUR PRODUCT

If you love Teslas, be a Tesla salesman. Don't be a Toyota salesman who drives a Tesla. You absolutely must believe in your product, and it must be of benefit to the people you are selling. If you won't buy it, why should anybody else? You may be able to convince someone by pretending whatever you are selling is worth buying, but it will be an uphill battle. People can feel and see through you.

Once you've narrowed down to a product, ask yourself the following questions:

1. Does the product have universal appeal?
2. Is it limited to a particular market?
3. Would you buy or use your product?
4. Would your client benefit from owning or having one?

I am in the land business because everybody can be a client. If I'm doing homes, approximately 65-70 percent of the American housing market in 2012 are already home-owners and may not qualify for a second home. With land, there is no qualifying, which appealed to me, and having an inventory of all price points makes everybody a possible client. (https://www.reference.com)

FIND IT AND STICK WITH IT

There are so many good opportunities out there, and it's easy to be swayed from one thing to another. This is a fault I see with too many salespeople. They're selling a lot of things at any given time or changing from one product to another. Choose something you believe in and stick with it. I'm a broker, so I can do mortgages, sell homes, do property management, and who knows what else, but it's a surefire way to lose my identity and my niche. I just focus on land sales and give it my all.

KNOW YOUR PRODUCT

Once you have chosen a product you truly believe in, know everything about it. If it is a product you love, it will be fun to do the necessary research. When you like a person you are talking to, don't you enjoy finding out more about him or her? Taking a class is always fun if you are interested in the subject matter. You should be eager to know more and discover more.

If, for example, you are selling a skincare product, know the ingredients, uses, correct application, etc. You may want to see the factory where it is being produced, know who's behind the company, and their mission (and that it aligns with yours).

You have to be able to dissect your product down to its components. Don't you give a better tip to a server who knows how to explain the menu and who's very knowledge-able and confident about his/her recommendations when asked? In other words, it's important to become the author-ity in your field. Know both the positive and negative, ad-vantages, and disadvantages. Attend seminars on the sub-ject. Once you have a thorough knowledge of the product, understand the industry, its marketability, and the value that it can give to your clients and, ultimately, you. Be the expert on its use, benefits, and weakness.

There should be no surprises.

Be the expert on how your product will benefit your cli-ent. If it's make-up, will it give them better skin? If it's a car, will it make driving safer for them? Will it save them on gas and maintenance? Will the vitamins you are selling make people healthier? Will it help alleviate their pain? With land, I know it will give my clients a more secure future, can serve as a good plan B (instead of going back to Mom and Dad) because I know that the possibility of paying off your house is much less than paying off a $20,000 2.5 acre parcel. Should someone no longer be able to pay their mortgage because they lost their job, got sick, etc., it only takes a few months before the bank starts foreclosure. If they own a piece of land, however, they can buy a trailer (or put up a tent) and park it on their own property. They will never be homeless.

The more you know, the more confidence people will draw from you. Business is a give and take. You should always strive to give more than what you take, much more. If you expect your clients to give you their hard-earned money, you better be worth it. Perceived value is determined by the client's perception of who is providing it. People will have no problem paying much more if you give them more than what they are expecting.

KNOW YOURSELF, WHO YOU ARE, AND WHERE YOU ARE FROM

I tried skincare products, which gave me the experience I needed in sales, but I should have recognized a few things about myself. First of all, I don't have smooth, perfect skin.

I'm also not into beauty stuff and I'm not the girly-girl type. Skincare is not something I thoroughly appreciated when I got involved in the beauty industry. I did go to the factory so I could understand exactly what I was selling, but I didn't enjoy the products as much as I should have.

One day, I was trying to invite a prospective customer to look at the product. She had lovely, flawless skin, and I definitely did not.

"Oh, are you using the product?" she asked.

At that moment, I realized I had a big problem. How was I (and why was I) going to convince somebody with much better skin than me to use the product I was promoting? Thinking quickly, I said, "You should have seen me before!"

It was funny but really awkward.

I had to face the facts: I was more interested in the money-making aspect of the business than I was in the products themselves. Thankfully, the owner of the company agreed that my strengths lay more in presenting the financial rewards of the business to potential salespeople than selling the products themselves. As a result, I began advising, and they started using me to present the opportunity nationwide.

I started making great money, but there were a few unforeseen issues I hadn't thoroughly researched. For one thing, the company was getting bigger in the industry, and the competition came after them. So did lawsuits by people claiming everything from allergic rashes to bipolar disorders caused by their products. After a few too many losses and lawsuits, the company failed. As a result of this experience, I realized that working for someone else wasn't ideal for me. I needed control, preferably of every aspect of the business, and I'd had little to no control at all. I also learned that I didn't want a salary for exactly the same reason—control. I wanted full commission at my next job. In that way, I would be completely responsible for what I earned.

KNOW YOUR COMPETITORS AND DIFFERENTIATE

If you've thought of it, most of the time, somebody is already doing or using it. You, therefore, have to be different and better. What will set you apart? Why should someone go to you and not your competitor? What's your added value? Knowing your competitors, anticipating changes in the market, etc., is of tremendous help to the company, to clients, and to your income. When you're talking about less expensive products, differentiation can be by appearance, price, options, and even flavor. There are a variety of different fast food places, but they manage to differentiate themselves in subtle ways. In-N-Out and McDonalds both sell burgers but somehow feel very different. Right? You go there for a particular burger, and you know exactly what to expect.

For me, after spending years working in the land business, I understood how most of these companies operate.

In general, they purchase large parcels, subdivide them, and then sell the smaller parcels. For the most part, huge parcels are only available quite far from development. This business model was, and is, efficient and makes for easy training and selling because it allows agents to bring busloads of people to the same location where the subdivision is located.

Over time, however, that business model began to nag at me. I realized that these particular subdivided parcels didn't always suit everyone's needs. I felt that clients might be better served by having the opportunity to own land in varying locations, in a variety of sizes, to suit their particular goals—not just ours as a company. Taking prospective clients to a given subdivision and selling each piece until they are all sold is convenient for the company and its agents, but not necessarily what was best for the clients.

Since changing the way an already successful business was done was not a viable option for most land companies, I started my own company.

Having researched my competition and differentiated myself, clients come to me with a particular expectation for quality, location, affordability, and, especially financing options. I strive to be the company that offers the lowest down payment (10%) and finances the longest (30 years) with no prepayment penalty. I'm proud there is no qualifying, and that we make exchange of parcels possible. We are not offering clients a $100 item that makes the decision process

easy. We offer a high-priced item that will need a long commitment from our buyers. Because of the leap of faith tak-
en by my clients, I think it's crucial to break from norms
and trends. In my business, staying privately owned makes
these various aspects possible and is one way in which I
differentiate.

TAKE PRIDE IN WHAT YOU DO

Having started our business in a 300 square foot room
where I was the janitor, broker, marketer, receptionist,
bookkeeper, etc., I learned every aspect of my business. It
is easy to justify all that is good because it is mine and to be
naturally protective, but I also understand the need to be
my best critic. I try to make honest dissections and analyses
of my business. I try to understand the ins and outs, the
pros and cons, the great and not so great aspects of what we
do. It is good to see and hear various points of view to make
sure I see everything objectively, so I do ask my children,
husband, parents, and trusted friends and clients about
how I can do things better. I ask for honest criticism and
comments.

We ask our family, relatives, and friends for advice because they care about us and look out for us. This can, at
times, be very detrimental, though, especially when it's
about career choice. Family—especially our parents— may
not always be the best resource. Nobody loves us more, but
there will be times when their fear of seeing us fail may

limit our ability to succeed or even try at all. As for our friends, it can be a mixed bag. Some may be envious of you succeeding, and others genuinely afraid of the idea of losing you to something bigger. Either way, they can subconsciously try to undermine your success. If you do need advice about what to do for a living definitely do not ask your neighbor - if they are so great and successful, they shouldn't be living next to you!

Whatever you decide to do, take the utmost pride in your chosen career. If you want others to respect and validate your choice, it has to start with you. In truth, your self-esteem and pride are the very best kind of self-promotion. If you're not proud of what you're doing, you shouldn't be doing it. Remember, many dabble in sales and don't succeed—you have every right to be proud that you're giving it your all.

5

Identify Your Market

HUMANS ONLY NEED THE basics to survive: food, clothing, and shelter. Beyond that, it's all about the need we feel—the things we want, desire, and believe we must have to make our lives happy. Sales, in large part, is about creating that need. The goal is to be in a business that is beneficial to most, if not all. The bigger your market, obviously the better.

I chose land sales, because to me, it is a product that has value for everyone and needs no explanation. There is no cultural divide. I do not need to explain how it can benefit anyone. There is no need to explain how and why—I only have to show where it is.

There is nothing new about land sales, and this particular transaction has been happening throughout history. If, in fact, it is a product that all understand and value, why then is land ownership only for the very few? Cost is one factor, but I have found that basic knowledge about the subject stops many people from even inquiring. If you don't know anything about something, you tend to shy away from it. Knowledge empowers people.

Early on, I put together a PowerPoint presentation that provides basic knowledge about land in the simplest way possible. America uses linear measurement (acreage) as opposed to metric (hectares) like most of the rest of the world. This, in itself, creates a disconnect and discomfort. I find that as soon as people understand the conversion, it is one of the biggest aha moments.

Once they are clear on the measurement system, I show potential clients an approx. 2.4 acre (a hectare) both as an empty lot and with improvements like houses and buildings. By explaining how land is parceled out and some of the basics in understanding how to buy land, I am able to help reduce the fear of the unknown and help potential clients relax.

KNOW YOUR CLIENTS

Who needs what you are offering? Who will benefit from your product or service but doesn't realize it yet? Who has the ability to buy your product? These are all key questions that need to be answered.

Let's use our car sales example. Pretty much everyone needs transportation, but you need to narrow down your most likely client base. What income bracket? What demographic? You need to talk to people who own luxury cars to understand what makes them buy one. What motivates them to own one? Is it prestige, safety, or both? Would they buy the same car or brand again? You need to know what makes them happy and sad about owning one.

In addition, if you are selling a luxury car, it may then not make sense to advertise in a penny magazine. You may want to network with higher-income people to promote your product effectively. You must choose the right events where you will meet the most likely buyers.

I have a company video, but I use a PowerPoint presentation because I can gauge and cater information to a particular client's personal frame of reference. I think of my clients on a scale of one to ten in terms of land knowledge. Doctors, for example, often know little about land, and are probably in the two range. However, a doctor who is already an investor is probably at about an eight level. When someone is at the two level, I gear up my presentation, but only to level three or four, otherwise, you lose them. When they're in the eight range, I have to be ready to go to a nine, ten, or even eleven in terms of the information I provide. When I am with developers, I have to be able to go even higher than that.

It is important to know the advantages and disadvantages of people from different walks of life. Approach each client with a fresh perspective because no two people are exactly alike. Giving a canned presentation is one of the worst things you can do.

Simply stated, know your client and tailor your presentation accordingly. I usually do this through conversation in the first few minutes I'm talking to someone. By asking questions, listening to the answers, and telling stories, I gain a bit of an understanding or window into what they want and need.

UNDERSTANDING DIVERSITY

There are over 100 countries, hundreds, maybe thousands of languages, and lots of different cultures. We do not believe in the same things and do not always do things the same way. Each of us that makes up the world's seven billion-plus population have different opinions and different ways of doing things. What motivates you may not motivate someone else. To expect others to totally appreciate your perspective on every topic is asking for trouble. If you are talking to someone face-to-face, remember you are looking at each other from different vistas, and there are various angles from which you can enjoy a particular view.

Be respectful of the differences and similarities between people. Research different cultures. Try various authentic restaurants. Food is something that is enjoyable to discuss. It will not only make dining more exciting but provide common ground.

A rainbow is breathtaking because it is made up of different colors. We are all different. We are products of different environments, and we are shaped by those life experiences.

This diverse country offers an opportunity to learn from people from very different backgrounds. Realization and appreciation of this fact will determine your success in sales. It will also make your job so much more interesting and fun.

IT'S NOT ABOUT THE SIZE OF THE SALE

The impact you make on someone who buys say, a small $15,000 parcel of land (or whatever you are selling) is way bigger than somebody who already has millions. Besides, that person could be so thrilled, they refer more business than whatever you made from a one-time larger transaction. It happens way more often than you'd ever expect.

To me, making people happy with my service is what matters. I have sold small, average, and big parcels to clients. My hope is to make a difference in their lives someday. I get referrals from my bigger clients, but the medium to average clients gives us the cash flow that keeps our doors open and makes our business viable even during recessions or pandemics.

Remember, ten dimes make a dollar. It's that simple. Always do your best with everybody. Be consistent. When speaking in a big group, make sure that you address the whole room, not just one side. When dealing with individual clients, always do your best presentation, no matter if they are considering a small or huge purchase. I make everyone feel important and treat them all the same-- whether they are buying a million-dollar piece of land or a $15,000 parcel. By consistently doing this, I have clients who call me back a few years after attending our presentation telling me they are now ready to purchase.

HAVE RESPECT FOR ALL

I make it a point to always treat everyone the way I want to be treated. Never ever think that you deserve better than others. If you want the best for yourself, your children, and your community, shouldn't others feel the same way? Realize that we all want to send our children to the best schools, give our family and friends the best we can provide, live in a nice home, drive a nice car, and travel to our favorite places. If anything, we must look after those who are not as fortunate or as strong.

I once made presentations to a group of very well-dressed city officials. One gentleman, who was seated at the back in a t-shirt and slippers, seemed different. After the presentation, the normal questions were raised. When everyone was almost ready to leave, he approached me with questions about a certain property and what I thought would be best for his budget—meaning he was interested.

The following morning, I was awakened by the hotel staff and found him waiting in the lobby with a cash payment for what I'd recommended.

Had I pre-judged, I'd have assumed he was the least likely, as opposed to the most likely to buy, and would have lost him as a client.

NOT EVERYONE IS YOUR CLIENT

No matter how strongly you believe in what you do, you can't convince everyone they need what you are presenting. No president ever gets 100% of the vote. Trying to get everyone to agree with your point of view is not only pointless, but unnecessary.

I respect those who prefer other forms of investment over land. Land is not for everybody. I have a stockbroker who is not invested in land. I, on the other hand, am not invested in stocks near as much as he thinks I should be. We have known each other for decades and remain really good friends. He gets his information about land development from me, and I get my updates on the stock market from him.

If everyone owns a home, who will rent from apartment owners? Some people are more interested in stocks than investing in land, and that's a good thing. We need investors in the stock market to drive our economy. I accept that I cannot convince everybody. I just do my best, give it my all, and leave it at that.

As long as you do your best at any given time, get ready to say "next!" I do not dwell on negative comments and never take them personally, only constructively. We may or may not succeed, but having tried and failed is way better than having not tried at all.

REFERRALS ARE THE BEST SALES

Talking about yourself is bragging, but having somebody else talk you up is the best advertising. If I say, *Jet can make thunder,* I'm bragging, and it's obnoxious. If somebody else tells you I can actually create thunder, it's a totally different story.

Print and other forms of media advertising may work, but referrals work best. If you are being referred by prior clients or people who know you, you have already cleared over 50% of the closing hurdle.

There are numerous land companies out there, but when someone comes to me referred by another client, I don't have to go through all the steps of introducing the company, myself, and then the product. All I have to focus on is what the person needs and how he or she can benefit from using my product. If for only this reason, we should be consistent and always take care of each and every sale we make. Throughout my sales career, I have had countless surprise referrals—incredible clients who've come from people I'd have never expected.

Most of my business comes from referrals, and it tends to come in clusters. For instance, I did business with a Laotian guy who was well known in the Laotian Community. He began to refer friends and relatives who referred more people. During that period of time, I started to feel like I was in Laos. I began to eat like a Laotian. The same has happened with a group of Japanese and then Italian people. My business tends to go that way—almost like a miner finding a vein of gold. I love it because I learn about other people and cultures while I teach them about land.

It is your job to live up to the expectation, and more. The reason these clients have come to you is because someone spoke highly of you and your product. Do not disappoint. Be more than what they are expecting. If you are consistent about treating all people well and deliver more than you've promised, the referrals will continue to come. You don't even have to ask.

VALUING RELATIONSHIPS

In any business, you need to network to find clients. Creating true friendships and valuing these relationships is the best thing I have done for my business. Clients who've become my friends are not only my best referral source but help me enjoy my life and career tremendously. To me, my clients are not just clients, I consider them my extended family and true friends. I never lose sight of the fact that they can buy land with another company, but they chose to do business with us. For that, I am always grateful.

6

Sales 101

WHILE IT MAY SEEM obvious, many potentially successful salespeople sabotage themselves by failing to recognize and adopt some basic (and not so basic) elements of good salesmanship. Potential clients are looking to you and at you as they are deciding whether to buy what you are offering. You owe it to yourself and to them to be at your best in a variety of different ways:

IMAGE

You need to determine the kind of image you want to project. It may feel awkward if that image is not how you are now, but keep doing it, and it will become natural in time without even trying. Dress for Success! While this can mean different things in different industries, figure out what you need to be wearing and rock it!

Using the luxury car sales example, you need to dress stylishly for the clientele you are trying to attract. Cosmetics sales require good grooming, skincare know-how, and a proficiency in applying make-up. However, if you are selling tractors and farm equipment, it makes a lot more sense to dress comfortably than it does to wear a designer suit. You'll look silly trudging through mud in fancy leather shoes!

To be at your best, you need to take into consideration the following:

- **Good Hygiene**—Most people are visual. We are told not to judge a book by its cover, but we all do. If you are clean and well-groomed, it shows discipline and respect for yourself and others. Nothing is worse than body odor or bad breath, so bathe, brush your teeth, and always have mints on hand!
- **Let the Subtle Things do the Talking**—The way you accessorize says a lot about you. People notice the little things, and they add up.
- **Project Confidence**—And not just about the product you are selling. Fake it 'til you make it if you have to! Be careful though—confidence must never cross the fine line into arrogance.
- **Mind and Body**—Take care of your mental and physical self with exercise, a healthy diet, and enough sleep. Self-care makes a huge difference that affects everything about you.

FIRST IMPRESSIONS

As the saying goes, there is no second chance to make a first impression. The sale starts with you. Your demeanor is sometimes all your potential client has to go on, so make those first moments count.

- **Shake Hands**—Not too weak and not too firm!
- **Make Eye Contact**—Eye contact is key in conversations. You may talk with your lips, but your eyes validate what you are saying. They also show sincerity and trustworthiness.
- **Smile** –It's your best accessory!
- **What's in a Name?**—I say everything! If you have a name that is difficult to pronounce or remember, you might consider a catchy nickname. I find that people remember me specifically because of my name. For one thing, they usually expect to meet a man (and it surprises them that I'm not), but I chose Jet because it was easily associated with something that moves fast—just like me!
- **Happy Disposition**—No one wants to be around someone who's grouchy. If you are having a bad day, don't impose your mood on everyone else. Positivity is a major attraction.

BE YOUR BEST YOU

We are all special, and it's important to know and tap into your best self.

- **Be There/Be Present**— It is enormously important to be in the moment. I turn off my cell phone when I am meeting with someone. If there is a true emergency, my staff know where to find me. Otherwise, the client I'm with has my full, undivided attention.

- **Dial-up your "Likability Factor"**—People want to do business with somebody they like. How do you make people like you? Find common ground, listen, and be the best resource for what they need. Use humor and laughter - it is the best ice breaker. Self-deprecating humor makes people more comfortable with you, and laughter, like food, is universal. Be ready to engage in funny conversations, but mindful of not offending anybody. And, always, stay away from religion or politics.

- **Be Inquisitive and Knowledgeable**—In addition to having a thorough understanding of your product, it is also important to have a decent understanding of as many issues as you can. Know what's happening in the community and the world. I make sure I read, listen to the news, and attend classes because information is food for your brain. It's important to have a passion for learning, be it through reading, watching, or listening. Having knowledge will help you become a great person to talk to.

I have to make sure I have in-depth knowledge and understanding of the most basic things about land. For instance,

I not only have to know that there are 43,560 square feet in an acre, but that I must know how it looks and feel when it is an empty lot, or when it is fully or partially built out. I am often asked how big some of the shopping centers that we see while on tours, and I have to be able to get a good guess of how big they are.

If you are in the restaurant business, knowing all the ingredients used, where they are from, why they are used is a must. If in the car business, knowing what kind of engine and all its parts, its advantages, and how it compares to your competitors will make your clients comfortable in dealing with you.

- **Engage your Clients**—Make it all about them. Use examples that are relevant to them or their business.

In my presentations, I use attendees' homes or their neighborhoods as an example. This makes it more interesting for them and validates what I am saying. I will ask for the size of their home, when they purchased it and for how much, and then break it down to how much they are paying in taxes. Most of us simply just pay our tax bills when due. Being able to make my client understand how their tax bills came about, and how they are computed, is always met with appreciation.

- **Compliment/Acknowledge**—Do not be stingy with sincere praise!

When meeting for the first time, I look for the positive in everyone (there is always something). I look for things that I can honestly compliment - their hair, clothes, shoes, etc. When in a conversation, if I notice a good voice, I compliment it. If they can give me a great answer to my questions, I make everybody aware, often by repeating it so everyone can hear.

WORK ETHIC

When you are in sales, your income is entirely dependent on how hard and how smart you work, so it is crucial that you make the most of every day.

- **Start Your Day Early**—I make calls, exercise, submit offers, and get the hard stuff done right off the bat so I can enjoy what unfolds from there. I find that taking on the biggest decisions and issues first thing is not only effective, but rewarding, as it makes the rest of the day easier, brighter, and more fun.

- **Compartmentalize**—Learn how to separate tasks in a way that best suits you. You may want to check your email at a certain time of the day, respond to calls in the afternoon, etc. Having a set pattern or schedule is one way to best manage your day and optimize your productivity.

- **Organization**—Your work area, for instance, says a lot about you. Because I am in the land business, I have many maps, pictures of development, brochures about land, and news articles around me. Make sure that it is organized and that it "speaks" of who you are and what you represent. Make your venue conducive to getting work done in line with your product. And how many times have you searched for your keys, which not only made you late, but worse mad? By being organized, it saves a lot of time and avoids unnecessary chaos.

- **Discipline—Have the ability to do things even with nobody watching.**

As my own boss, no one will tell me what time I need to get out of bed and start working. Allocating time wisely is a must. Just because you own your own time, it does not mean it can be wasted indiscriminately. Having a clear goal of how much you should be making in an hour, a day, a week, or a month will help you manage your time most effectively.

- **Take Initiative—**Do things not just because you have to, or when someone tells you to. Take matters into your own hands.

If my agents have too many in the group to tour, he or she doesn't need to ask. I will be there to help out.

- **Punctuality—**There is nothing worse than starting a meeting with someone by making an excuse about why you are late. It is always best to be ahead of time. If you are speaking/presenting outside your office, get there early. It gives you time to prepare all your materials and equipment and get a feel of the venue. It also gives you the chance to greet, meet, and know people as they come.

- **Avoid Procrastination**—It is much easier to deal with whatever needs to be done than to procrastinate. If it is too big a goal or project, divide it into smaller, manageable pieces. In this age of technology, that also means you need to step away from social media and other distractions. Social media may be a great way of connecting us with friends, but do it in a way that you do not needlessly squander one of your best assets, your time. Focus instead on your personal growth - being more knowledgeable with your product, being the best presenter, etc.

- **Always Strive to Do Your Best**—Put value and importance on everything you do. Set high goals and commit to meet those goals.

- **Focus**—We are constantly bombarded with choices—work or stay home, be happy, or be melancholy. We choose what kind of milk, cheese, dressing, even what kind of sugar to have in our coffees. America abounds with opportunities. Because we have so many options, it is sometimes almost impossible to not have doubts about the choices we make. It is easy to think that other businesses or career paths are better. But, as the saying goes, the grass always looks greener on the other side of the fence. That is until you are the one tending it. The truth is, to have the perfect grass, you need the right watering, fertilizer, and care.

- **Consistency**—It is key in whatever you are doing and pays off.

- **Work Really Hard**—It makes playing hard a lot more fun.
- **Stay Hungry**—Complacency and contentment will get you nowhere.

7

Pro Tips

AT ITS CORE, sales is about finding a need and filling it. If you have a new product to offer, it is your job to make your client see how that product is of value to them. If you take care of people's needs, yours will automatically be taken care of.

Sounds easy, right?

Actually, it is, but you may have to master a few vital skills which don't always come naturally.

VALUE YOUR TIME AND BE MINDFUL OF YOUR CLIENTS' ALLOTTED TIME

Time is a valuable asset we are all given for free. How you manage and make use of your time is what will determine whether you succeed or fail. Do not squander time. We are all given 24 hours in a day. It doesn't matter if you have a Timex or a Rolex, it will be the same 24 hours for us all. It is a good reminder that everybody is on an even playing field when it comes to time. It is the ability of successful people to leverage and manage their time that will make the difference. Always value your time and that of your potential clients.

Make a decision as to how much you should make in a month, in a week, in a day, or in an hour. It will give you a goal to shoot for and exceed!

When doing a presentation, show up on time and always let everyone know how long it will take. After thirty minutes, you start losing your audiences' attention. If, however, what you are saying is interesting, relevant, and fun, they will be engaged and ask questions. As a result, it will be worth everyone's time to continue on.

MASTER THE ART OF LISTENING

When you are speaking, you are imparting what you already know. By listening more than speaking when you first meet someone, you will learn a lot about that person. The first three minutes is very important in gauging your client/clients. By listening, you gain a better understanding of what your clients need; hence you do not waste their time, and they don't waste yours.

If we were to drive somewhere together, and I ask you where you want to go, isn't it best if I find out where you want to go before I start driving? If I do not wait for your response and simply take off to where I assume you want to go, I may head in the wrong direction, wasting gas and both of our time.

MIRRORING

Finding commonality with others is extremely important. If I'm meeting with a prospective client who takes notes, I will grab a pen and paper. If he or she speaks fast, I try to talk at the same speed. If someone tends to put their hand on their chin, without even realizing it, I will oftentimes end up doing the same thing. I find that it helps create a bond. I used to be self-conscious about mirroring others, but now, it has become automatic.

It also helps to know who you are meeting with and have an idea as to what they do, if they have kids, etc. For instance, architects generally understand land better than, say, doctors, so I make adjustments in the way I conduct the conversation accordingly. You'll find the most productive meeting of the minds if you are on the same page. This is not to say you are faking who you are. Never do that. You are simply meeting people where they are at.

BE YOUR CLIENT

Do you like it when a salesperson is aggressive and pushy? Very few of us do. Make people feel comfortable with you by treating them with respect and deference.

I had an experience when buying a car when I was asked for our driver's licenses. The salesman refused to give back our licenses until we talked to the salesman, then the manager, then another manager. It was a very unpleasant experience. So unpleasant that not only didn't we buy from him, but we warned some of our friends about the dealership.

I have clients who felt they were not given the chance to do their due diligence or that they had several different salespeople trying to close the sale when working with other land companies. They appreciate our way of informing them of what we are offering and why we believe it's worth their consideration, and that it is ultimately up to them to decide. This way of selling helped us earn numerous repeat buyers and many, many referrals.

Just mentioning at the beginning of my presentation that land is not for everybody, makes my audience comfortable.

CHARACTER SELLS

Unless you have invented a totally new gadget, you probably are selling something that has been offered before. A person may do business with you if you are the cheapest, but you will make a lifetime client if you build a friendship. Sales is not just about price—it's about the relationships you forge as well as the trust and accountability you bring to the table.

LOVE YOURSELF

I grew up with a mom who told me to love myself. I didn't really fully understand what that meant at the time, but as I've gone through life, the message has become clearer. You cannot give what you do not have. You cannot water a plant with an empty bucket. Too many times, we are nicer to others than ourselves. We dress up nicely for other people, and use better towels and dishes when we have visitors. Why not use the best for yourself? It will elevate your standards to the point where you will not have to make an effort toward others because it is simply who you are!

When you know who you are and love your authentic, original self, you will always be the best version of you.

NEVER LET ANYONE SEE YOU SWEAT

The old deodorant commercial is right! If you seem nervous, you will make your client nervous. You can easily lose a sale by showing that you are uncertain or afraid. The way to counter this fear is through practice and preparation.

• **Never Pitch From a Disadvantage**—Get very knowledgeable about your product, believe in it, and make sure you know more about it than your client.

• **Do Not Lose Your Cool**—I don't allow myself to get rattled by someone talking a lot or being disruptive during my presentation. In fact, I use the situation to my advantage by listening to their questions and paying attention. I find that they simply want to be heard or given attention. If you do this respectfully, you will eventually make most people your allies.

• **Be Adaptable**—Do not fight the flow. Things happen. A client's needs and preferences will sometimes change at the last moment. I do not let changes in meeting times or tour schedules affect my day. If it is canceled or rescheduled, I simply work on other tasks that need to be done.

- **Multi-task**—Be ready to apply different skill sets at all times. Though we have staff assigned to specific tasks, I have to be ready to fill in when there is a need. If an agent or broker fails to show up or needs assistance for a scheduled tour, presentation, or paperwork, I have to be ready to step in.

NEVER SAY BAD THINGS ABOUT ANYONE

Like the old saying goes, if you don't have something nice to say, don't say anything at all. When you say something bad about someone, it haunts you. Even if the person you told says nothing, you have created doubt and fear. Avoid gossip at all costs. When someone starts talking to you about other people, change the topic. They will only do it if they have an interested audience. Talk about the weather, your kids, travel, etc. instead. Saying negative things about your competitors will not make you look any better. There are bullies on every playground. They are just competitors protecting their perceived turf. Let them talk about you, but ignore anything they say. You do not get a better reputation by stepping on someone else's. Find the positive in people. Mostly, people are good - you just have to dig deep, really deep, for some.

- **Limit Negativity**—Do not spend as much time with naysayers, negative people, or whiners. If you have to, because they are family or very close family friends, make spending time with them allow you to appreciate your positive friends, and make them the best guide of how not to be. Finding the positive in people and the best in everything leads to a happy existence.

PRACTICE WHAT YOU PREACH

I will not sell a product I do not use or own. How can you explain the benefit of something truthfully or exude confidence about its value if you have not used and benefited from it? I will not tell people to own land if I do not own any. Even if you think nobody knows, YOU know. The belief has to start from within. Nowadays, information is available at the click of a button. Be truthful, and you will make sharing with people a whole lot easier.

SENSIBILITY BEATS SENSITIVITY

Sales is a numbers game. Everything is. The more you do it, the better you become, and the easier it gets. Heightened sensitivity is detrimental in sales. You've got to learn not to take any of the NO's personally. I do not dwell on negative comments, and never take them personally, only constructively. People will criticize and rain on your parade. Be strong when this happens. Don't allow your feelings to get hurt. No matter how you try, there is no way you can please everybody. Stay on course, and continue to do what you know is right. It is on the hard transactions and difficult situations that we learn, and become our best. It is all those rejections that make us better at what we do. The key is learning about why and handling the word *no* to eventually get more of the yeses.

HAVE MENTORS

Have as many mentors in life as you can. We only live one life, but having mentors gives us the knowledge of having lived several more. You will not only gain a wider perspective and an understanding about things, but consulting with others who know more may just help avoid unnecessary mistakes. It will simply make you better at what you do.

One of my mentors owns a lot of land in California. When I was looking into buying land he said, "Jet, in San Diego, you'll forever be the smallest fish and you'll get eaten for lunch by the bigger fish. What you do is you look for a small lake where you can be the biggest fish."

At the time, all I could afford was a dry lake, but I made it work!

Remember though, no matter how much time you spend with your mentor or reading books to gain knowledge, up until you decide to do something, nothing will change. In the end, you have to take action on what you've learned.

INNOVATE

Always be on the lookout for how to make things better, more efficient. There is always room for improvement. Do not be complacent. Be a solution provider.

Technology had been a great help in my industry. We now have websites and applications that can make researching a property's terrain, ownership, size, etc. easy and we train our agents how to use them. Since it's easy to pinpoint a property's location using satellite imagery and GPS, some clients are already sold and don't feel the need to go on a tour to visit the actual parcel. These days, sharing of news and information is made way easier through different social media platforms. I take advantage of that so that my clients and agents are easily updated about our industry.

HAVE A PHILOSOPHY

My philosophy has remained the same since we started: To only sell parcels I am willing to buy myself. Secondly, I always do my best to see matters from each client's perspective.

Figure out your philosophy and live by it!

ALWAYS SPEAK YOUR TRUTH

Truth is easy, simple, and uncomplicated. Stick with what is true to you. If you always have to convince yourself, you may be headed in the wrong direction. Right decisions are easy to make. When it is making you think twice, stop! It is when you have to wrangle within yourself that you should take a second look.

When a lawsuit was filed by a client whom we had to cancel for nonpayment, it was not something that kept me awake at night. I will not do anything illegal or anything that would harm the very people who put food on my table. They were most likely hoping that we did something wrong and that we had something to hide. Having tried diligently to do business the right way from the get-go, I was afraid of nothing. I was willing to risk it all. I was warned that there's no guarantee about the outcome where legal battles are concerned, but decided to fight the unfair lawsuit to the end anyway.

Other than the outrageous expense, it was all worth it. It is indeed during these trying times that you learn the most valuable lessons. Education may indeed be costly, but ignorance will cost you more.

DO THE RIGHT THING

If you need to justify any decision, consider that it may not be the right one. If it is making you contemplate, it is not a good sign. Always be accountable. I do full research and due diligence on any property I offer because I buy it first. If I were just brokering, I wouldn't have to because I don't own it and haven't spent any money on it. At the end of the day, I'm not perfect, and mistakes have happened. For instance, I sold a piece of land that had an undisclosed issue we discovered when a client was ready to build. I had it reviewed by various reporting agencies and the utility company. Upon confirmation, I offered to give a full refund or an exchange. Because the client hadn't gotten exactly what he and I both believed he had paid for, I took the plot back and offered him a better piece of land. Being able to do right by him made both of us feel good about doing business together.

Having learned such issues could happen, I now do an extensive review on all parcels we have for sale. For an added precaution, I make sure that I have 2 to 3 parcels that the company would own and never sell on all areas where the company offers land. This will be the best assurance that I can provide our clients.

Always strive to be better. Be your own competition.

8

It's All in the Presentation

BEFORE I DO a presentation, I try to do a little mind exercise. I will go in a room, bathroom, my car, or anywhere I can be alone to clear my head. I owe it to people attending my presentation to do my best. I continue to learn, and become more prepared each time.

In sales, you have to be able to justify the *what* (for me: land), *why* (best speculative investment), *where* (the area with the most potential), *when* (now—assuming the client is ready), and *with whom* (with Capital Holdings, of course!)

When I begin my presentation, I start with the big picture and narrow it down from there. Because I am selling land, I point out that it's the most valuable thing anywhere in the world.

Where?

The United States, because it has the biggest economy in the world.

California is the most populous state in the U.S with the biggest economy amongst the fifty states. Why is it the biggest economic state? Because of its location, which makes it the port of entry for all businesses and goods coming from the Pacific. What are the next most popular states? Texas, Florida, and New York. What do they all have in common? Again, they are the ports, but California, is number one, because it alone controls everything from the Pacific Rim.

I have all the visuals in my offices in my conference rooms, including world maps. I also have a PowerPoint presentation that I can adjust if, for example, a client is from the Philippines.

In that case, I will ask, "Do you ever wonder why we have more Filipinos here?" and then explain that it is because we are closest to the Pacific, closest to our hometown. It's as simple as that, but it gives credibility if you can then support it with facts. I really like it when I have millennials. They fact check everything I'm saying. I'm very visual, so I need the world map and other materials to confirm my words.

Having narrowed in on California, I then point to the fact that Southern California has approximately 60% of the state's population.

In other words, I connect the dots for them not just by explaining, but with a visual.

If they are from Los Angeles, I ask, "How much is the land in L.A.?" and then give them an advertisement of land for sale in their area. If they are coming from Cerritos, I have land prices in that area, too.

At that point, we all agree that land is good, but that there is no way they can afford the price of land where they live.

I make sure I make my audience members participate by asking them questions about land where they live, or by using their home as an example to determine the land price in their area. Knowing how much it is in their area encourages them to realize that the possibility of owning land may only be achievable in a newly developing area.

Given what I have learned with research, time, and experience, I definitely know now that it is possible to own land at almost any budget. It may not always be feasible in already developed areas, but we do have a chance to own and afford land in upcoming and developing areas.

I find that if I clear up the *What, Where,* and *Why,* the *When* and *With Whom,* are the easiest hurdles to clear.

My presentations are normally on weekends when prospective clients would usually be spending time with their families. Instead, they choose to spend their free time with me. I am very respectful of this and try my best to educate, give them a fun time, and send them away having learned something. I have to make sure that I have given every attendee something that will be valuable to them now or in the future. More than anything, I want them to be empowered.

In order to make every presentation of consistently high quality, I always do the following:

PREPARE IN ADVANCE

I make sure that I have all materials, information, and the appropriate parcels that will meet the budget and needs of the clients organized in advance. I make sure all my equipment is in working condition and test everything the day before. I do research, know my facts, and check my sources on all relevant information for attendees.

I developed my presentation based on what I would want and need to know if I were the potential client. I look at all the preparation I do as creating a library full of materials I believe other people need to know or might be interested in knowing.

You will not convince someone who sees you with no teeth. In other words, always be ready, and prepared. Have all the tools at your disposal, but use only what you need.

KNOW YOUR CLIENT

Before someone comes in, google them, look them up on social media, make sure you know exactly how to pronounce their name, and ask questions to whoever referred them so you can adjust, conform, and know where to focus to make your time with them most productive. I don't go into the very basics about land with someone who is an engineer, architect, or builder because they already know what I'm telling them. On the other hand, I may have to go into more detail with a teacher, accountant, or a dentist who understands everything about teeth, but little about land. Of course, I will not have the opportunity to give them all that I know at one time, but that's where analyzing and understanding what your attendees need to know and hear comes of importance.

- **Determine who the decision-maker is in the family and make sure he/she attends**—This simple tip will save you lots of time, and time is money. If possible, have all the people that will be part of the decision making process present – spouses, kids, the accountant, and even their fortune teller!

- **Find out what the client needs, not what you want**— We all want to make a sale, but your desire is not what will make it so. Don't assume you know what is best for someone. Your opinion is not what matters. Present the information properly and let the client decide what is best for them. If you find out what they need and give it to them, you will both get what you want!

- **Qualify Your Client**—They say sales is a rejection business. It does not have to be. If it is, you may not be qualifying or doing things as you should. You may be offering something that people may need and like, but cannot afford, or you may be offering something to someone who absolutely has no use or need for it. Make sure to identify your market correctly. For instance, I do not offer a million-dollar property to somebody with an income that cannot support such a purchase. You will waste your time and their time. If you analyze and qualify correctly, you will decrease your rejection ratio significantly.

PUT ON A PRESENTATION PEOPLE WILL REMEMBER

- **Make the subject interesting**—People assume presentations are boring. Prove them otherwise. Make teaching about your product factual, interesting, relevant, and by injecting funny stories and involve them by using the client's situation or need in your examples.
- **Know your facts and check your sources**—I have printed material to back up what I am saying. Clients will trust what you are saying more if someone else says it too. You can do this by using news articles, showing video clips, giving them a website to check, etc.
- **Keep it simple**—More is not necessarily better. Colored maps don't necessarily translate to more sales.

Streamlining and making a presentation concise can help anyone better comprehend a new subject and see how it applies to their situation. For example, in almost every presentation for clients unfamiliar with a land investment, I will commonly ask attendees the size of their house lot and the age of their home to determine how much the value of their land has increased (as opposed to the actual home structure.) I urge them to take a look at their property tax bill, and, sure enough, they will report that the increased value of their home is significantly tied to the land itself. This type of revelation is helpful in getting people to understand that investing in real estate is more than just buying homes and leasing them. It helps them understand the inherent value of land alone.

- **If you don't know the answer, do not guess**—It is better to say, "let me find/research the answer to that, and I'll get back with you as soon as possible." More important, do get back with them - even if you do not make the sale.

- **Inform and educate**—Don't "sell." Make it a conversation more than a presentation. Empower people by teaching them about a subject and it makes the decision process easy. If you do this right, you never have to sell.

The best sales are done when the client actually sees and realizes the need for your product themselves. Figure out what your client actually wants and why. **Take note of what your client says during your meeting**—Repeat some exact words in answering their questions. It will show you're listening and that you are on the same page.

ELIMINATE RISK

The inability to make a decision on the part of your client is normally based on perceived risk, which could be the price, reliability of the product, and other factors. You can mitigate risk by providing as much information as possible. You can reduce the perceived risk substantially by the added value you offer. Remember, it is not always just the price, but the value that matters.

- **Know What to Do and What Not To Do**—The fact that a potential client made an effort to meet, means you have to make it worth their time to make them feel comfortable and welcome. Ask questions. Listen when they are answering your questions. Don't interrupt. There are various angles where you can enjoy a particular view. Where you are facing is the opposite of where the one you are talking to is looking. What motivates you may not be the motivation for others.

- **Price**—I do thorough price research and have ads with prices from my competitors. In addition, I take into consideration a potential client's ability to afford my product. I ask many questions, including, *what would be a comfortable long term payment that you can afford without pulling food off your table?*

Because I am selling a long-term, costly item, I make sure people understand that they are not purchasing a liquid asset, they can just turn around and sell on a whim. Just like any form of investment there are risks. Just like buying stocks or a home, you have to be able to weather a recession. You don't want to sell when prices are down. The key is, will you be able to keep your payment up until the market recovers? By doing this, I am also "buttoning up" my sale and avoiding needless cancellation.

- **Give the information and justification the best you can**—If you do, there will be no reason why they will not want to do what you are suggesting.
- **People Want to Buy**—The act of "buying" is one of the most joyful things we do in life. We all want to buy a house, a car, clothes, accessories, etc. "Retail Therapy" is one of the best ways to cure boredom and costs much less than a human therapist. All that is needed is a justification of why he or she should. Make them want to do it with you!

KNOW WHEN TO CLOSE

Stop repeating yourself. Stop talking and go for a close when you should. If you're doing it right, you're closing all the time. You don't do a long animated sales pitch and then try to close. You do mini-closes as you go along, otherwise, you risk not closing the deal because you've oversold and people are already bored to death. Some people are already 90% there when they show up, and all you have to do is figure out the justification as to why without going through the whole spiel. It's up to you to notice the cues and don't oversell.

- **Ask Closing Questions**—Throughout your presentation, you should be asking closing questions. After each closing question, stop and wait for a response. Do not fill the silence with endless chatter. Wait - no matter how long and how uncomfortable, for the answer to your question. I find that in these situations, you lose if you are the first to speak.

- **Finish ahead of time, if not on time**—Leave your clients energized and enthusiastic, not bored and exhausted. Make them want to come back to you the second, third, or all the time.

PROVIDE LOTS OF FOOD

It is next to impossible to close a transaction when people are hungry. Provide drinks, snacks, and more snacks. Providing food shows thoughtfulness. It is also a great source of endorphins!

PRACTICE MAKES PERFECT

Practice, practice, and more practice. You may not nail your presentation on your first few attempts, but you will get better each time. Every setback is an opportunity to learn and be better next time.

Expect to be flooded with questions, especially if the audience perceives you have limited knowledge or are new in your craft. Make endless presentations, and you will most likely have heard it all. Having given the chance to answer most objections repeatedly, you get better and better at answering them.

I do a lot of presentations. Having done them so many times makes me better at my craft. I have been asked a lot of questions and encountered objections in so many different ways that I feel ready for whatever is thrown at me. I still get nervous prior to each presentation, which I believe is a good thing. It keeps me from becoming complacent.

Time and practice give you the confidence that people see when you speak. Interestingly, I've discovered that the more experienced you are, and the more you know, the fewer questions are asked, maybe because you anticipated the normal questions/objections, and you have already addressed them in your presentation.

If you keep doing what you are doing, you'll find ways and hacks on how to do it better, easier.

If you want it, work for it.

9

Client Interaction

EVEN IF YOU ARE offering the best product in the world and your presentation materials are beyond first-rate, you will lose sales if you don't know how to share that knowledge with potential clients in an intelligent and effective manner. How you interact is just as important as what you are selling.

In order to maximize the percentage of deals you close, you need to be aware of and engage the following strategies:

LISTEN

I keep bringing up the art of listening because it is so important. When you are speaking, you are imparting what you already know. It is when you listen that you learn. When you listen to what your clients are saying, it gives you direction about where to go, what to say, and gives you a better understanding of what they need. I truly believe the best way to effectively close any deal is to stop talking and start listening.

AGREE BEFORE YOU DISAGREE

Never say to a client that they are wrong outright. Allowing people to voice their thoughts and opinions is what attracts people to you. If there's something that people have in common, it is the need to be right. Do not immediately shut down somebody's idea. Hear what they have to say, agree that it is a good issue, compliment them for bringing it up, and share where you are coming from. Putting people in a corner makes them defensive, and gives them a reason to build a higher wall—a wall specifically designed to keep you on the other side.

When someone comes to me saying that land is not a liquid investment, I agree first, by saying, "That is so true," but then I add, "And, by the way, that's what makes it a good investment. It is something that you cannot easily decide to give up on a whim. It forces you to stay on it, which may give you the most benefit."

GIVE EVERYONE THE BENEFIT OF THE DOUBT

Never assume that somebody will or will not love your product. At times, people come in who seem to be disinterested about land (especially the young millennials who are dragged in reluctantly by their parents). That is until I start making the presentation in a way they can understand and relate to. Talk the "language" of who you are presenting to. The sale often hinges on your ability to connect and explain what you are offering.

BE OPEN-MINDED/DON'T BE JUDGMENTAL

If you are in sales, you don't deal with just one kind of person. Relish that. Depending on what you choose to sell, it can give you kind of big scope in terms of clientele. I have clients from many different cultures. I have clients who want to do cleansing rituals on their parcels, or want to make sure their land is facing east, etc. I had one client who sent a "mind doctor" to a huge parcel he was considering. The gentleman stood with his eyes closed in the middle of the land for nearly an hour. Aside from worrying about the summer heat and his being attacked by wild coyotes, I sat in the car and let him be. If someone is interested in a property, I welcome them to do whatever they need to do to be certain about their decision. In the case of the "mind doctor," it was an easy sell. I did not have to do any convincing at all. All it took was his okay on the property, and we signed the paperwork.

Remember, there is no single way to look at or do things. Everyone has the right to their ways and their opinions— respect theirs, and they will likely respect yours.

PATIENCE

Not all clients are the same. Some are easy to teach, some a bit slower. Have the patience to treat everybody accordingly.

I am always ready to make a detailed presentation to our clients. It is a bonus if, during the conversation, I find that it does not have to be that detailed. Some people get the point really fast, and some folks need to have everything explained in detail. My clients are from different cultural groups and some, like myself, count English as their second language. I try to separate my meetings if there is an obvious difference in my clients' understanding of the subject. If it's not possible to do so, I make sure that no one is left out by engaging the knowledgeable one to help explain to those who need a little bit more information. This works really well.

CREATE TRUE RELATIONSHIPS

I consider this the best of the many perks in my business. Not only do I thoroughly enjoy meeting people from different cultures, but it also gives me a much better perspective and appreciation about a lot of things.

I find that creating true relationships not only offers amazing personal growth, but it also is the best asset your company will ever have. Happy and satisfied clients will always be your best advertisement.

IMPOSE AND YOU LOSE

Never force a sale. You would not like it done to you, so never do it to anyone. Be respectful. Never ever make it all about you!

Though the basic necessities of life—food (grown on land), clothing (harvested from material grown on land), and shelter (atop land)—are all somehow related to land, I simply make sure potential clients see the relevance of owning land. Deciding to own that land must be my clients' choice.

DO NOT GET OFFENDED EASILY

Not everybody will be, and should be, your client. If, after having done your assessment of your product to a prospective client, you don't see the benefit for them, let go. It is an unnecessary burden for both them and you. If there is no need, it won't be long before your client realizes it, and will forever resent having bought from you. On the flip side, turning away from a deal that will not benefit your client will come back to you tenfold.

One could argue that creating a need is what a salesperson does. It is true in a way, but the key is letting go when you know it will not benefit that person. If you can, make your detractor your ally. Sometimes they have a valid issue. If so, it may be worth looking into. If they are only trying to get attention, walk away. There are seven-plus billion people in the world. It's not worth the energy. Those who have a full appreciation and need for your product will make your business grow.

ASK FOR FEEDBACK

Ask for comments and evaluation whenever you can, especially when you do not make a sale. If you can't get the input you need, always "rewind" and see where you might have made a mistake or where you could have done better.

HANDLE BUYER'S REMORSE IN ADVANCE

Don't you occasionally feel remorse after you purchase something? We all do. You may be able to lessen potential feelings of remorse by addressing this head-on after you make a close by reminding your clients that they may feel butterflies in their stomach once they are home, have a family member or a friend who may not understand the benefit of having this product and therefore may not agree with what they have just decided. Give them scenarios that may come up after they go home so that once they are in bed and really start having that butterfly sensation in their stomach, they will be comforted by the fact that you forewarned them of this, and it will help make their buyer's remorse that much more tolerable.

You may not be able to save all your deals this way, but that is part of being in sales.

WHAT YOU DO AFTER THE SALE MATTERS A LOT

Once a sale is made, it is critical that you follow up. Have thank you cards ready and mail them promptly. When you follow up, make sure your clients are satisfied with the product you sold them and that it is working as promised. If need be, offer to show them again how it works or how to use it. We provide a monthly newsletter to update our clients about what's happening in the area. If a client calls, make sure that they get a call back promptly. Our staff is ready to help them whatever they may request – their account balance, transfer of ownership, change of vesting, etc.

Always appreciate the fact that though they could have done business with someone else, they chose to do it with you.

DON'T BURN BRIDGES

It is important to let people who don't buy know they can always call you when and if they are ready. Sale or no sale, always end up on a good note. You never know when you're going to meet someone again.

If clients are not ready to make a decision when they first see me, that is ok. I find that if I've done what I was supposed to do, they are usually lacking the down payment or need to straighten up their finances. We make sure that attendees get the monthly newsletter, greetings from the company on holidays, etc. By doing the best presentation I can at all times, keeping in contact, and providing them relevant information, they do call us later when they are ready. One client attended a presentation a number of years ago, and, on her birthday, decided to purchase a property as a gift to herself.

SAY IT. MEAN IT!

Don't make empty promises, especially to yourself. Maybe no one else will know, but YOU WILL! If you cannot trust yourself, who can? If you know you can't or won't do something, don't say you will.

Nothing makes you lose credibility and respect more than saying things you do not mean. As I've said, it's always better to under-promise and over deliver.

10

Building a Team

AFTER SPENDING YEARS DEALING with other people's property, I had the opportunity to help people become landowners. It was a challenge I enjoyed taking on. However, I had to build and maintain a sales force from scratch.

How?

In all my business ventures, I prefer making people want to work with me, not for me. I spend most of my waking hours with my staff, so it is crucial that we enjoy working with each other, have each other's backs, and share the same vision. It is amazing how working with a team you trust, and respect makes running a business so worthwhile.

In order to create this culture, I developed my team and hired new people based on the following principles:

DESIGN YOUR BUSINESS FOR THE LONG TERM

Understand that whatever you do today will have implications for the future, and can affect your clients and everyone in your team. Try to do things right. Don't take shortcuts. Don't jump into quick fixes. Address issues when they happen instead of putting it off for later. Hoping that issues would simply go away will compound its complexity instead. I intend for the business to continue long after I retire, so I am always mindful of the impact that any action or decisions might have in the long run.

BE A LEADER

There is no need for a fancy title. People follow those who have the capacity to lead. Make people want to work with you, not for you, by setting the best example and working the hardest. Do everything the same way you expect your employees to do. Also, be open to criticism. It is an opportunity to learn how to be better.

KNOW AND UNDERSTAND EVERY JOB

Be ready and able to take on whatever you ask from everybody in your team. There is nothing better than a leader who knows and understands what it takes for his/her staff to do the task at hand. Starting as my own janitor, clerk, accountant, marketer, and errand person made me well prepared in many ways, particularly concerning hiring needs. This knowledge is also very important in formulating the processes essential to having a successful business. Each part of the process must be duplicatable, and everybody needs a clear understanding as to why they are doing what they are doing and why they are a relevant part of the whole process.

DELEGATE

Just because you know how to do everything yourself doesn't mean you should do it all. Even if it were possible to handle everything, neither you nor I are the best person for every task. I recognize that there will always be someone who is better than me at any given activity, and I must know what and when to delegate.

CREATE A DUPLICATABLE SALES PROCESS

Be able to train others to do the task. If I have multiple appointments, I have very capable people who can step up to the plate in my place.

CROSS TRAIN YOUR STAFF

Life happens. People get sick, emergencies occur, and it is not acceptable for clients to have to wait to have their concerns addressed until the one person who knows the answer to a particular question comes back.

MAKE YOUR PRIORITIES CLEAR
TO YOUR EMPLOYEES

Mine are integrity, honesty, and success through hard work. My staff is like family to me. Because they know who

I am and where I stand, they hold themselves to similar high standards. It is not unusual for my staff to get commendations from our clients and people we work with. They understand that service to our clients is of utmost importance.

BE DECISIVE.

TAKE RESPONSIBILITY. BE ACCOUNTABLE.

In life, decisions must be made. I find that the right decision is easy. If a decision requires you to lose sleep, give it thorough consideration--it may not be the right one.

If you are struggling, I suggest making a T bar to help you with your decision where you write the positives of a situation on one side of the T and the negatives on the other. Writing the pros and cons of every decision you want to make makes the choices clear and easy.

If you make a decision and it ends up not being the right one, own it! Use making decisions, whether right or wrong, an opportunity to learn. I do not necessarily make the correct choices all the time, but I've learned that the key is to make more right than wrong decisions. Looking back, I think the wrong decisions I've made were actually the stepping stones I needed to increase my odds of making the right ones. Nothing is worse, however, than not making a decision or allowing someone else to be the reason why you will or will not do something.

ELEVATE AND APPRECIATE

People say, *it is lonely at the top.* It isn't if you take as many people with you as you can.

MAKE *THANK YOU* YOUR TWO FAVORITE WORDS

Always give thanks and acknowledgment where it is due. Always thank people along the way. It is your experiences with others that made you the unique person that you are now. Offer sincere praise and compliments—especially to your staff.

OWN UP TO YOUR MISTAKES

Mistakes are an essential element of growing up and a path towards perfecting your processes. Failures are the most valuable learning opportunities. Errors equal growth. When you make a mistake, accept responsibility. People who blame others for their mistakes may think that they are making themselves look better. On the contrary, it makes them look weak and cowardly.

"Sorry" is a very powerful word, and it has the vast ability to save you a lot of heartache. Nobody is perfect. No one! Pride will cost you pain. If, like me, you have been guilty of having to be right and prove others wrong, let go! Apologizing will not diminish you in anyone's eyes. Instead, it will earn respect.

ATTITUDE IS CONTAGIOUS

Notice that when you yawn, people around you start to yawn? Your attitude impacts the people around you. If you exude joy, people will emulate your mood. Have a bad attitude, and it spreads even faster!

People gravitate toward those who are happy, fun to be around, and smile, so laugh at yourself and do not take yourself too seriously. I believe you should make giving hope to others your responsibility. Be the reason that somebody smiles each day. Acknowledge people. Hug whenever you can—it is absolutely good for you.

Above all, try to have fun in whatever you do - lots of it! I make sure that I have as many belly laughs as possible each day.

BE FAIR

Nothing is harder to deal with for staff than an inconsistent boss or one who plays favorites.

Though people have different predicaments and circumstances, we have to make sure that we have policies that ensure fairness for all.

LET OTHERS SHINE

You don't need all the glory. Let the success of others reflect on you.

Nobody gets anywhere without the collaboration of other people in one's life. Giving recognition to those who helped to make you who you are will not only encourage them to work with you, but will give you fulfillment as well.

LOYALTY WILL GET YOU FAR

When you are loyal to your employees and treat them like family, they stick around and treat you with the same respect.

Everything starts with you - if you give loyalty to people you work with, you will get it back tenfold. Loyalty is not something that you can demand from people. Loyalty is earned.

It gives me the best feeling of gratitude that our staff will not even question if they have to stay after office hours, or come on a weekend if needed.

When we were in litigation, it was heartwarming to have so many clients and people we do business with write commendation letters, and be willing to testify on our behalf. It had a huge impact on our case.

SHARE, GIVE, OFFER, PROVIDE

I believe that selflessness is the most gratifying experience you can give yourself. Never be stingy with what you know, or what you have - it will create a bigger space for you to receive more in abundance. Take care of others, and you will be taken care of without even trying. Make being useful to others, your community, and your world your ultimate life goal.

Nothing makes me feel happier than being of help and benefit to others.

SEVER RELATIONSHIPS WHEN YOU MUST

Cutting people out of your life, whether professionally or personally is rarely pleasant, but must sometimes be done. Accept that this is a cost of doing business. Aside from family, you have a choice as to who you want to be in your circle, who you want to be your client, and who you want to work with. It is one of the perks of being an entrepreneur.

SHARE YOUR VICTORIES

I am totally aware that wherever I may be in life, I owe it to my family, the people I work with, and people whom I have met. I am a summation of all the people I have known. All the successes that I've had were made possible by the people who have shaped my belief. There is no such thing as success without the help of others. Never forget that it is impossible to do it all yourself. I am forever indebted to the people in my team. They will always be a part of who I am.

11

Persistence, Motivation, and Compromise

OVER THE YEARS, I've sold pastries, cosmetics, opened a clothing boutique, and much more. It is because I've worked in, or run, so many different businesses in the past that I have full appreciation and understanding of what I do now. I was even bankrupt at one point. I cried and wallowed in self-pity for more than a few days, but my three children gave me the strength to get up and not give up until I found the right industry and business for me.

Loving what I do keeps me motivated. So does knowing there are more talented and hardworking people out there who have to work harder than me to provide for their families. I know I have been given a chance, and I have no intention of wasting the opportunities I've been given. Knowing my reason and my endgame makes me want to go to work to do what is necessary to keep our business going.

Why are you here? What is your motivation in life? If it is to provide for your family, you are off to a good start. It is extremely important to have goals—both for the long term and how you want your day, month, year, and life to be. Just like consulting a map before going on a road trip instead of setting out without direction and reason, it is far less chaotic to have a plan.

EXPECT AND BE READY FOR CHANGE

It is true that change is the only constant in this world. It is no different in business. Be open and expect change. Just because you have been doing something a certain way doesn't mean there is no better way. Like a palm tree or bamboo, be pliant and go where the wind goes. Adjust and conform. Flexibility and the ability to go with the flow is a necessity in this world. Things can always be improved upon. Welcome change—embrace and celebrate it. Accept that change has to come to make things better.

When I prepare for a presentation outside my office, I am ready for all that might happen. I test all my equipment, but I am always ready with my visuals in case my equipment fails. If the venue changes at the last minute, I make sure that I have all that I need to make the switch. For a while, the Coronavirus outbreak made in-person presentations impossible. We had to adapt quickly to give presentations online, modify the way we show properties, and make all the necessary adaptations for reopening. The pandemic made wearing a mask on our tours and presentation a must. I now use a microphone during presentations to help my audience hear me clearly. I have walkie-talkies spread out in the convoy of cars when we tour. I even created video tours for those that do not want to venture out, but want an idea of what the area looks like.

While it's been a challenging time, some of the modifications we've made have been so effective, we are implementing them permanently.

OBSTACLES AND CHALLENGES ARE PART OF LIFE

It is easy to question why you are going through some challenges, but all it takes is to look around you. You need not look far to see that other people are faced with way bigger challenges and much bigger crosses to bear.

In business, obstacles and challenges are a given. Worrying is a total waste of time, and it is never productive. All you can do is anticipate the best you can, have faith, the willingness to do what is necessary, and you will get through the hard times just fine. Conducting your business honestly gives you the best protection.

While I was fighting the lawsuit filed against us, I dealt with various unpleasant emotions. Looking back now, it could be one of the best lessons in my life. In business, anybody can sue you. I learned that greed can make people lie and believe their lies. They can call you any name they want. All you can control is how you react to whatever is thrown at you.

If you are worth anything, you may be sued. If you can, budget for that eventuality. It is just part of doing business. If you know you have not done anything to be sued for and you are sued anyway, congratulate yourself! It means somebody perceives you to be worth something. Otherwise, why would they bother?

I think of obstacles this way: when there is construction on the highway that causes you to be stuck in traffic, why not look around instead of being frustrated? They are probably widening those roads for a reason – population increase, which means probably a good location to consider owning land.

Rather than getting mad, get even and buy land!

WELCOME REJECTION

Never forget that rejection is your best ally, there to make you stronger. If you know what you are selling to a client will benefit them, do not take anyone's rejection personally. It is them letting go of the opportunity you are presenting. As I've said, everyone should not be your customer. I see rejection as a challenge. I actually enjoy it. I ask myself, what did I do wrong? Where did I fail? What did I not do? There is no *poor me*.

Always analyze and gauge the things you did or did not do, especially if you failed to close a deal. What could you have done to end up with a positive result? What could you have done differently? What did you miss? Be your own best critic by analyzing what went wrong and just say *next*.

SAVE FOR TAXES AND RAINY DAYS

Being in sales and being an entrepreneur means accepting both feast and famine. There will be times when you will make unprecedented sales, but there will also be times when nothing happens at all. The best way to make a sale is when you do not need to--when you are not worried about you, but have the best interests of the client at heart. I make it a habit to set aside fifty percent of what I make, more if I can for the lean times. Having enough set aside makes life in sales so much easier. Less stress equals more sales!

STAY BALANCED

Have a good handle on the emotional fluctuations inherent in sales and entrepreneurship. Have time offs. Take a break. Eat healthy. Gets lots of sleep. When having a rough patch, get away, walk, run, do something else different. A rested mind gives a better perspective and focus.

PERSISTENCE

Success takes making calls, endless touring, building meaningful relationships, making sales presentations, reading, studying, strategizing, delegating, and following up. I know that I must have the discipline and self-control to do what is necessary to get things done. I have toured some parcels many, many times to a multitude of different clients. I never give up knowing that I will eventually have the right buyer for it.

I have one parcel that had a portion with a hole on it. Though it was a nicely located parcel, prospective clients would ask why? What happened? Because I couldn't determine the reason, I would sometimes joke that maybe Superman landed there. After several tours, one buyer saw the parcel's location as an advantage despite the hole. He bought it, and, eventually, made a nice profit.

FAILURE

Though I always expect the best, I am also ready for the worst. When I make a sale, I am ready should it cancel. I will always do my best to save a deal, but I also know that it is a numbers game. Early on in my career, I made nine sales in one day. I went home spending the expected money in my head - what bills to pay, things to buy, etc. However, before the three-day cancellation period passed, I received a call that all nine of my deals were canceling, not to mention two more (the ones who'd referred me to the nine now-canceled deals). I definitely lost sleep that night and for a few more nights after that, but having gone through the experience, I learned to never count my chicks before they hatch.

SELF-CONTROL

It is easy to get frustrated when things don't necessarily go the way you want them to.

I find that it helps to remind myself that I have no control of a lot of things that can happen each day, and that I can only control how I react to them. It helps me put things in perspective. In addition, I try to have a grasp of how I feel at all times. I do not let the weather or opinions of others make the decision of how my day is going to be.

I know that I must have the discipline and self-control to do what is necessary for things to get done. I enjoy watching movies, but I know I have to get to sleep early when I have a tour or commitment the following day. One habit that has helped me a lot is always having my sales materials ready before I go home. It has happened too many times that I get an unexpected visitor, builder referral, etc. Being ready has helped me avoid unnecessary stressful situations.

BE REALISTIC

Success means compromise. When we started, our business took up almost all of our weekends and our free time with our children. Having our parents help us out made it easier. Still, it was time that I can never regain. Know what it takes, how much sacrifice and hard work it requires. Inaction will never get a positive result. Action does.

ENJOY THE JOURNEY

It is never the destination that defines life. Embrace the entire journey, and you give life its real meaning! Let life shape you. You can reflect on the past, and consider the future, but make sure to prioritize and be on the present. There are phases in life – the accumulation phase, and, later, the giving or sharing phase. Do not settle for just taking care of yourself. It is when you give that you totally enjoy success.

Your level of appreciation about everything around you is a total reflection of who you are. This creates a deeper sense of calm and enjoyment that makes you a person that people would want to have around and want to do business with.

Appreciation is the key to happiness.

12

Live Your Best Life

WE ALL AIM TO get from points A to Z. Our means of travel will determine how fast we get to our destination. We can walk, run, bike, drive, or fly a rocket ship. Choosing the right career can offer us the mode of transport most suited for the journey. Because life is not all about how fast we get there, but the experience itself, it is critical to understand if it is the speed at which we get to our destination, or the journey itself that makes us happiest. Maybe it is a combination of both.

I've spent the bulk of this book talking about sales, so I thought I'd wrap things up with some other thoughts that have given me a framework to live and work by. I believe it has led me to where I am today and allowed me to live a fuller, happier, more meaningful life.

EVERYONE HAS SOMETHING TO OFFER

Everyone contributes to your life experience—be they somebody we aspire to be like or the last person on earth we would want to become. I learn and expand my knowledge through everyone I meet and everything I do. I am the person I am today as a result of other people making me a part of their lives, too.

OPPORTUNITY IS EVERYWHERE

Vast opportunities are all around us, but most of the time we are too busy looking elsewhere and miss the things just waiting for us to grab right in our midst. We feel the need to travel when there is so much to enjoy just outside our window, in our own backyards.

Life happens around us every second, minute, every hour. There are so many things to learn and enjoy. It could be getting pleasure in watching people, having a meaningful conversation, enjoying the view. All you need to do is pay attention, focus, and have fun. Too many times, we look forward to what might happen and fail to enjoy what is happening.

Celebrate milestones along the way. It's not just about reaching the top of the mountain to enjoy the view. There is just as much to see and appreciate along the way.

TAKE TIME FOR YOURSELF,
FAMILY, AND FRIENDS

Make sure to allocate time for yourself, family, and friends. Your parents will not always be there. If you have kids, they cannot put growing up on hold up until you are ready to spend time with them. It is easy to justify how busy we are because you want to make things better for them. No material thing can even come close to the value of time spent with your loved ones. Success later in life will be much more meaningful if you have your friends and family to share it with.

UNDERSTAND THE POWER OF GIVING, THE GIFT OF SHARING

You are the lucky recipient when you give. Selflessness is the most gratifying experience you can give yourself. Be a source of love and abundance.

Still, we all want to have a nice home for our families, send our kids to the best schools, have a good retirement, etc. If you are one of the lucky ones who is given the opportunity to achieve all that, be there to help others who are not as fortunate. Be ready to take responsibility for others who are not able to take care of themselves. If you are given the talent and blessings, share them. A cake tastes best when eaten with others. Eating it by yourself will not only make you fat, it will make you diabetic!

It is sometimes daunting to think of what you as an individual can do or if an idea you've had will even make the least difference. I say, do it anyway - if each of us does just a little, we will all have a lot more than we need.

Be appreciative, thankful, and grateful. Nobody owes you anything. When you learn to be grateful, blessings can be boundless. Being thankful for what you have instead of agonizing over what you think you ought to have will allow you to enjoy your enormous life.

BELIEVE YOU CAN, AND YOU WILL

You will never travel the distance without first believing you can. Having faith in what you can do is a must before you can convince others. Your mindset and clarity of purpose are imperative to your success. Everything starts with you, so never stop dreaming.

I always pictured having a beautiful home for my parents, working in my own office, managing my own business, and being able to help others. These scenarios played over and over in my mind. At first, I kept a lot of these thoughts to myself, but eventually, I shared them with the people who mattered to me. I believe having a clear vision of what I wanted, and sharing my hopes and dreams aloud, set my mind and body in motion and enabled my dreams to become reality.

YOU ATTRACT POSSIBILITIES IF YOU EMIT THEM

Provide possibilities for people, and your life will be full. Be happy for others - be truly happy for the success of others. Try to make a difference to all you meet - be it with a smile, handshake, or a positive thought. Do not just use up space, but rather create and improve space for others.

LOVE WHAT YOU DO

Love what you do, even with its imperfections, or find something else that you will. There is no life rehearsal. Make this your best life!

TODAY IS THE DAY

The fact is, tomorrow will be the day that you will wish that you'd done it today. Though there is no going back to yesterday, you have the power to make each day forward your best.

LIFE IS LIKE A SLINGSHOT

I draw similarities between life and a slingshot, one of my favorite toys growing up. The more you pull back, the further it goes. In life, the more setbacks, the better prepared you are to handle challenges. To do so, you may need to change your attitudes toward:

Rejection--make it your friend.

Doubt--no more!

Self-worth--never compromise.

Faith--keeps you grounded.

Inquisitiveness - you'll only get your answer if you ask.

Family and Friends--make it all worthwhile.

Love--have lots of it!

Money--can be used for great things.

LIFE IS ALSO LIKE A BASEBALL GAME

Do not let anybody's action or words stop you from achieving your dream. It may take several attempts to reach your goal, but keep going. There will be hurdles along the way that will test your resolve, but just keep going anyway. They will eventually be a great necessity – making your destination that much more worthwhile, more meaningful. If you are absolutely happy where you are, do nothing. But if you want life to be different, do something.

Notice that people in the bleachers watching the game are the ones who ridicule and boo the players? Just remember that they are also the ones who are paying to watch the players play. Don't mind what detractors are saying, be in the game, and you will eventually hit a home run. Keep swinging and keep taking (calculated) chances!

KNOW YOUR TRUTH

The *truth* can be totally different from one individual to another, depending on their experiences. Hence, there are all kinds of religions that people claim or believe is the "ultimate" truth. As human beings, we feel a myriad of emotions every second, minute, or hour of the day. We may even evolve into a totally different person as we age. You may be a drunk in your thirties and might change your ways after a bad kidney or liver diagnosis in your forties and no longer drink and live the healthiest lifestyle. Your friends from in your thirties are stuck with the notion of you being a drunk, and your friends from in your forties may even consider you the guru of healthy living. As it is, our truth also changes through time, but so as long as you are true to self, life should be more meaningful.

If you are going to be in sales, or on whatever career you choose, it will be best to be your true, happy self.

FINAL THOUGHTS

I hope this book has resonated with you and that it has opened your eyes to see how easy and fulfilling a career in sales, and being an entrepreneur can be. The financial rewards can be great, but creating an overflow so that others may share what you have accomplished is what life is all about.

Along the way, don't forget to laugh, enjoy, and maintain a sense of wonder in this awesome world full of opportunity. It is not always about the money. It never is, and never should be.

Sharing this opportunity with others is not only rewarding, but something I absolutely enjoy doing. Loving what you do, and looking forward to going to work every day, is the key to achieving true wealth.

www.ingramcontent.com/pod-product-compliance
Lightning Source LLC
Chambersburg PA
CBHW050526190326
41458CB00045B/6721/J